A Welcome Shore

Also by the author:

The Roar on the Other Side
A Guide for Student Poets

Sketches of Home

What a Light Thing, This Stone

Weather of the House

A WELCOME
SHORE

Suzanne Underwood
RHODES

canonpress
Moscow, Idaho

Published by Canon Press
P.O. Box 8729, Moscow, ID 83843
800.488.2034 | www.canonpress.com

Suzanne Underwood Rhodes, *A Welcome Shore*
Copyright © 2010 by Suzanne Underwood Rhodes

Several pieces from this book first appeared in the following publications, some in a slightly altered form: "A Glimpse" in *The Sow's Ear Poetry Review* (published as "Shelter"), "Shenandoah Dreams" in *64 Magazine*, "Advent" in *What a Light Thing, This Stone*, and "Raggedy Ann on God" in *Shenandoah: The Washington and Lee University Review*.

Author photo and interior photography copyright © 2010 by Wayne Rhodes
Cover and interior design by Laura Storm
Cover photo copyright © 2010 by Janna Golovacheva

Printed in the United States of America.

Library of Congress Cataloging-in-Publication Data

Rhodes, Suzanne U.
  A welcome shore / Suzanne Underwood Rhodes.
    p. cm.
  ISBN-13: 978-1-59128-074-3 (pbk.)
  ISBN-10: 1-59128-074-5 (pbk.)
  I. Title.
  PS3568.H665W45 2010
  811'.6--dc22
                          2010013377

10 11 12 13 14 15   9 8 7 6 5 4 3 2 1

To Wayne,
my true love

CONTENTS

Acknowledgments   9

Foreword   11

1
SHORELINE

A Glimpse   15

Cold, Soaking Skin   17

Mountains and Sea   19

Touches   21

Signs and Wonders   23

Morning Shower   27

New Address   29

First Snow   31

Notes on Today   33

Ocean Calendar   35

Without the Cherry   37

Tangier, Virginia   39

2
TRIBUTARIES

Shenandoah Dreams   47

Mr. Boh and Bela   51

House on Hatemonger Hill   53

The Third Day of Spring   55

Scrapbook Pages   57

The Heart Has Its Hunger   63

3
CHANNELS

Wonderful Hand   69

Aunt Claire   71

Watermarks   73

Her Grandmother Lillian's Gown   75

No More Rabbits   77

Johnny   79

O. D. and Ruth   83

All That Jazz   87

4
TIDEPOOLS

The Soul's Blood   91

Broken Teeth   93

Lethal Shadow   95

Tangy Chermoula   97

URL-Y to Bed   99

Where Music Comes From   101

Glass Music   103

Waxwings   105

Frown   109

Mermaid's Tears   111

Heart Hollow   113

A Royal Season Mixed with Myrrh   115

ACKNOWLEDGMENTS

I wish to thank the following individuals for their generous and expert help.

To Doug Jones, for inviting me to write this book and for his invaluable suggestions.

To Laura Storm, for her energetic and encouraging spirit, her nimble acts as a liaison, and her gift of friendship.

To Larry Richman, beloved friend of many years who, as a seasoned editor and writer, gave up many hours to read and edit the manuscript.

To Wayne, my talented husband, for his contribution of photographs and for our treks up and down many welcome shores.

To the Lord, my Heavenly Muse, whose gift of words gives great joy.

FOREWORD

It is an ongoing wonder when a writer is able to infuse her prose with such poetic quality and tenderness that each piece becomes a poem in itself. Suzanne Rhodes has this magical facility of seeing to the heart of things, so that in her brief narratives each little hook for the imagination is a small pixel that adds to the whole and, in an observation, makes of complexity a simplicity that sticks in one's mind. She paints color and texture with words so that it all adds up to such a truth that I wonder why I hadn't come to the same conclusion on my own, in a similar circumstance.

But of course, no circumstance is identical to any other. Even the following day—same time, same place—the wind will have risen or the clouds have cleared, or a tight bud has just unfolded.

To retain the precision of the moment, one has to be there to experience it. Suzanne is a friend who takes my hand and says "Look!" or "Listen!" or just "Stay here with me while the meaning of this beauty unfolds." It's in that particularity and specificity of Rhodes' seeing and speaking that a comparison with Mary Oliver's writing becomes consistent in my mind. Both have eyes wide open for beauty and the significance of earthy things like shorelines and sedges, shells and what Suzanne calls "the slow simmer of time."

Her subjects include things like the miracle of the human hand, the tang of a marinade, how improvisational prayer is, a horse-shoe crab, or the weight of wetness on a morning tent. And much, much more—each sample a small slice of a life lived well, in which we are invited to join, powerfully moved, weeping or rejoicing with the writer.

Luci Shaw
Bellingham, Washington

1
SHORELINE

A GLIMPSE

It's 8 a.m., and I'm driving to work in my aging Buick station wagon, feeling displaced among the faceless cars. Before this life on the expressway, I lived in a town with a view of mountains, with neighbors of many years, with time to walk on land. Now I live close to an ocean that calls to my depths, but I spend hours on asphalt traveling to and from work and driving my daughter, Emily, all over creation. It's disheartening, the endless blocks of oversized stores, the blazing traffic. Everything is altered following a divorce. Moving away from all my connections, I live in a smothering fog. I picture myself as a goat in a fairy tale, caught in a sack.

Something catches my eye—a glint of water by the road. Like a secret within the marsh grass stands an egret, holding its curve against the deafening rush of time.

• • •

It's Wednesday and I've called in sick. I struggle to get out of bed. Can't eat or sleep. Objects make me nauseous—the door knob, the clock. The floor frightens me with its sloping and shining. Fragments and images swim through my head—Gregor the beetle stuck on his back, waving his extremities; Zelda Fitzgerald painting her strangled flowers. I spend the day crying. I tell God over and over what I tell him. I call my sister. She orders me to see a doctor, fearing I'm close to a breakdown. I obey. The doctor prescribes medicine. Over time I find my foothold.

• • •

I have a new friend named Wayne who rides to the beach with me. I like his dry humor, Texas accent, crinkly eyebrows. We ride our bikes past the fishing pier to the inlet at the boardwalk's end, then all the way to the other end where the hotels stop and the homes begin. I feel the ground beneath the wheels. I smell the salt-washed air. I like glancing back and seeing he is there in his red fleece and cap, with the sky and sea as background. It's all I need, a glimpse, a momentary shelter.

COLD, SOAKING SKIN

We got to the site at dark and I forgot how to pitch my tent and could barely see but I heard the ocean across the dunes and knew we were between water and woods. We can do this, I told her, as we fiddled with cords and nailed our stakes. But the sand gave way, and she said she'd sleep in the car—understandable, but a wincing reminder of breakage. I made the tent work, sort of, and crawled in to hear what I'd come for, the sweeping peace of waves, rustle of grasses. During the night the tent grew heavy with dew and fell in on me, a cold soaking skin, but I managed to push and prop it enough to keep it away. I slept until I knew it was light, then wormed out of my lean-to and saw the young world spread out all blue and white and singing, and the joy of it caught in my throat and I had no words for my astonishment. I let her sleep, my dear daughter who has no words for this grief, as I gathered wood from the other, shaded side for our fire that would burn off the chill and remind us that we are survivors and so much more, even when God seems far.

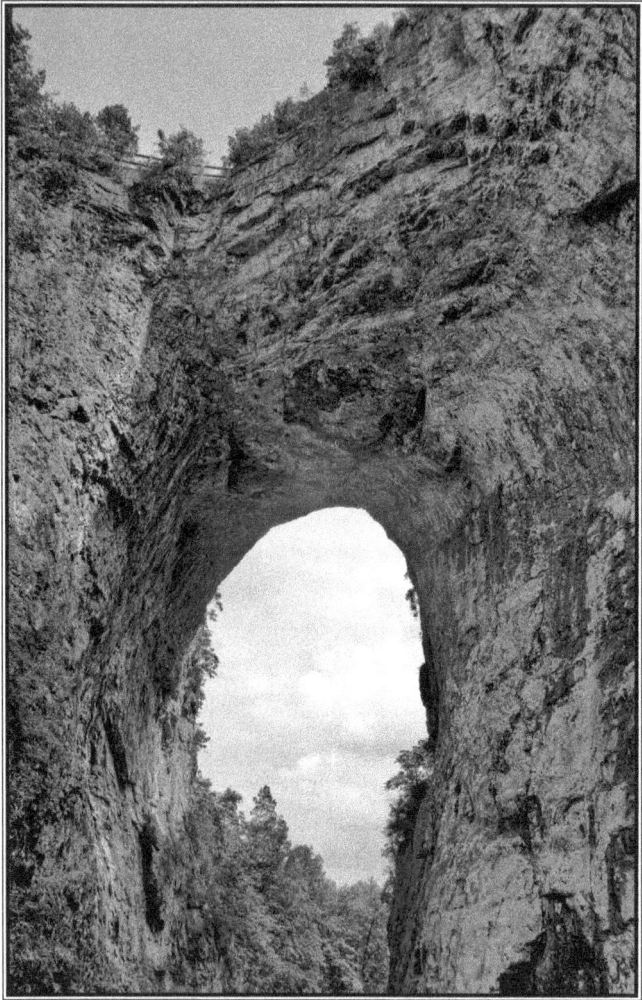

MOUNTAINS AND SEA

In the mountains I learned strength, to exert myself against stone, to find light in the closed-in spaces. How sweet the windfall apples on the Roan. From a high ridge we sailed paper airplanes down. We turned over rocks in the creek and watched armored crawdads clash against the breach. As darkness fell, the trees released owls in a gray shawl of wings.

I learned too that mind is mountain and words are handholds to take us up to purer air. When they were small, the children and I played with words limber as willows, fat as plums. We wrote poems and bounced sounds. We coined, we rimed, we colluded, collided. We climbed. We read for hours, even as daylight thinned and our stomachs growled, the four of us bundled together on the couch as we soared to galaxies of peril and adventure.

Later, I acquired other students and with them at King College, grappled with grand and difficult books like *King Lear, Frankenstein, The Fall*. My mind grew strong, just as taking four flights of stairs to my office in White Hall toughened my stride.

But this does not mean there wasn't much to crush a woman. My house was the mirror of a dying marriage. Ivy twisted through cracks in the cinderblock, and cave crickets like frog-sized horrors sprang out of the basement's dark. During storms, rain gushed in at ground level, and there was always a kind of seepage at the heart of the house that put me on edge, a damp uncertainty as I tended soup or made the bed or went upstairs to soothe a child's fretting.

The mountains taught me belief, for there they were, part of the sky itself, never moving. I must also admit to days, to years, when I never saw them at all.

· · ·

But now I have come to live by water—to let, to launch, to loosen. How am I to understand the way water, the mystery of created water, is forming me in mid-life?

Had I moved to desert or suburb or farmland, I would be someone different, even as the mountains did their work of shaping. Geography, the spaces on this "pale blue dot," cannot be understood apart from each of us in relation to the place where we have been set down, for the world was made the home of man and woman.

· · ·

My new husband and I ride bikes on a gravelly path that cuts through Back Bay. We pedal through a skein of dragonflies. I glance back and catch his eye. The turtles look up from the water.

Passing through pine trees and shadows, through Wash Woods—an extinct settlement formed by shipwrecked survivors with only a remnant church steeple to mark its place in the world—we come to a rise, then a sudden continent, a secret ocean spreading silver before us, and we dismount and tramp through the sand to take it in. We are the sole humans looking out from this spot, a brief and glittering forever sealed unto us without a word, with only my hand pulsing in his.

TOUCHES

His hand, like a bird's wing, brushes my face, traces my features. This new way of being loved makes me tremble and leave my shame.

I watch an old videotape of myself and feel embarrassed, for that woman caught on camera reading her poems in public seems, by her body language more than her words, to be saying, "I'm sorry to be standing here, so visible and vulnerable, but perhaps you will find value in the poems of these moments."

I read somewhere that existential shame is the psychological counterpart of an autoimmune disease attacking the body. Shame strikes at the self as if it were an intruder, a mistake. It stems from a spirit crushed by oppressive people who seek to expose, belittle, destroy.

This is different from the shame that follows moral transgressions. Shame was Peter's friend when he denied Christ, for in that terrifying anagnorisis when he saw his own Judas self, when the accusing, mountainous waves rose over his head, he felt the strength of a rescuing hand and let himself be taken. Shame was healed by love's touch.

My friend Linda rubs oil into the scalps of women at the Home for the Unwanted in Calcutta—one by one, the long row of strangers. As she works, she tries to rub out thoughts of what might be hiding in the close-cropped hair of those frail castaways who have been given shelter. In these intimate encounters with the poorest of the poor, she is changed forever.

I, too, have stroked the skin of the dying. It was my own mother, her smooth, bare back. Surprising, how young her skin felt as I said with my hand, "I'm here."

Love is the hand that finds what needs touching.

SIGNS AND WONDERS

When Wayne and I sit by the water's edge on a summer evening, letting the wind loosen our crimped nerves as our eyes adjust to the deepening light, that's when we see them, the pinpoints. Here and there, in and out, the black dots on eyestalks of *Ocypode quadrata* are sizing up their adversaries. Now and then, tiny detonations of sand occur near our toes as the ghostly tanks emerge from their burrows, pincer claws raised, battle-ready. They are but one of a host of signs and wonders shown us by our God when we're at play.

Inexplicably, on our honeymoon in Costa Rica, everything I wished to see was granted. "We've been here several times but we've never seen the promised whales," a man said to us during a sailing and snorkeling excursion as his wife nodded in agreement. That too was my longing. There we were, a high-spirited group in swimsuits, motoring away from the cove at Playa Buena past Gorilla Island toward farther waters of painted fish. Observing a long, dark line on the water, I announced to Wayne, "That is a whale." Sure enough, the line rose and grew into the grey cylindrical form of a fin whale, as the captain described it. The whale only partially surfaced, but everyone on board caught a magical glimpse.

More magic followed. We sailed to a small island and disembarked to explore a cave. Picking our way among the smooth, wet rocks, we noticed our guide bending down to gather something out of the shallow water. It was a spooky, spidery form the size of his hand, and he allowed it to crawl all along his arm. Then he fetched another for someone else to try. That would be me. I was surprised at how gentle the creature felt as it moved atop my hand, even as I wanted to fling the snaky arms back down to the stones from which they came. I had an epiphany on the spot about facing fear or maybe it was that things that look evil aren't necessarily so—I don't quite remember. I did find out later it was a black brittle starfish I held in a cave in Costa Rica, stranger than any star I'd ever seen.

Then there was the wish to see a snake. We had risen before dawn to be picked up for a morning hike in the rainforest by a young man named Eduardo who worked as a naturalist for a local tour company. On the way, we made a few stops overlooking fields and hills where our binoculars revealed two kinds of toucans (bright-billed and chestnut-mandibled) and various colorful parrots. Then we stepped into the forest, guests to its gradual light that gave us glimpses of tanagers, seedeaters, mot mots, guan—a turning kaleidoscope of whistles and hues.

High in the treetops, a troop of black howler monkeys made a row. They are the loudest land animals and can be heard three miles away—quite a contrast to the torpid lump of a two-toed sloth seen farther along. From hanging bridges, not for the fainthearted, we viewed waterfalls and a vast green extravagance, as if the earth itself were being born in this throbbing, voluble place. Wanting to see a snake was only fitting. Thus, when Eduardo stopped on the path and called us close, I saw my prize with joyous trepidation. Embedded in a bank of earth lay a coral snake, its red touching yellow (kill a fellow). It was more than I could have hoped for, to regard in perfect safety something so beautifully venomously itself upon the earth, a mere arm's length away.

Pleasures were always finding us—rain moving in the dark while we slept at Tabacon, first a gauzy drizzle, then drenching and soon departing sheets; the winks, hums, and chirps of myriad insects, the sudden eruptive boom of the volcano outside our very window, the warm slope of Wayne's body. If stars could sing, these would be their songs.

Looking out on the patio as I write this from home, I see the hanging flower basket with its hidden nest and house finch. In the overhanging wisteria lies another nest, this one belonging to a dove. Bumblebees float among the blooms. Privy to secret life, I am rich. Lord, keep me from the poverty of habitual sight.

MORNING SHOWER

I brush my teeth and watch his morning shower, the steam in-
fused with the lime-fresh smell of soap, his skin glistening in the
water's massage as he works shampoo into his scalp and rinses,
then brings the spray to a halt and stands scrubbed before his mir-
ror, catching my eye with his blue eyes, my toothpaste melting.

NEW ADDRESS

Since leaving my house in the Tennessee mountains, I've been through four moves, and before the mountains, I'd lived in thirteen different states. My latest home is a gift from my husband, who designed and built it. Not everyone would use my word palatial—in fact, one lady (the sort who would be found at a Jay Gatsby party) called it "a cute little house." I feel the way Moses, a student of mine from Nigeria, said he felt upon his first trip to an American supermarket: dazzled.

Does the new house call to me? my friend asks. Yes, but incrementally. It's a lot to take in. The homes of my past were modest and took work to make beautiful—a series of nameless apartments with thrift store couches; a house with gray walls; another with only one grate for heat. There was a house I loved on a street once lined with elms. Built in the 1920s, it had plaster walls, French doors, hardwood floors, doves nesting in the eaves, and children running up and down—but over time it sagged and declined with disrepair and growing leaks and cracks. I had to leave.

And then there are the houses of recurring dreams—vast and crumbling structures with endless rooms, unkempt beds, twisting hallways.

I remember all these houses but forget them, too, as the song swells. Every day I hear it as I unwrap china and oversee placement of new chairs and chests, as I fold my clothes into drawers. I hear it calling in columns and crown molding, arches and golden sconces—Wayne's poem to me, this house of his making with a room of my own for writing, a room that makes words possible, with shelves to hold all the companionable books that have followed me through my wayfaring, a wood stove for taking off the morning chill, and windows on three sides to let in light from the north, the south, the sea.

Yet I know that home is much more than structure. It's a lighted space where neither rage nor secret indecencies can breed. Home is an address, the original word meaning "to make straight," as in, to direct a message to a destination. But I think of it in another sense: at my new address, in the straightness of my husband's words and in his proven gentleness, the old serpentine strategies enacted in times of war—survival skills like hiding, covering, resisting—are slowly and finally unwrithing.

FIRST SNOW

Huge, gusting snow ghosts aloft today, cheerfully haunting the neighborhood. Snow at last—it's been six years. Wayne and I pile on layers of clothes and drive in the truck to the seashore park to hike in the woods across from the bay. We trudge past cypress trees standing in brown slush and see snow caught in the beards of Spanish moss. We hear bright chirps from a loblolly pine. We pass a man and a woman on skis, or rather they pass us. Another man is riding a bike and says he has snow tires! I like the cold snow on my face and the way we hold gloves and share our first snow world together.

NOTES ON TODAY

The big event at Mill Dam Creek this morning was a pileated woodpecker. Just a block from our house, the creek is a finger of Broad Bay that is an arm of the Chesapeake. Water, marsh, and woods conjoin and teem with birds of every sort: white-throated sparrow, belted kingfisher, red-winged blackbird, hooded merganser. But today it was the big woodpecker with its blood-red hammering head that drew the lenses of Wayne's camera and my binoculars. Seeing together on Saturday morning makes a lovely wedding.

• • •

Our afternoon spectacle was at the beach, a sponge-fest attended by a massive, cacophonous assembly of ring-billed gulls. Not only mounds of sponge but fish, too, had been left by a receding tide and were being devoured by the gulls and sanderlings. What a table set by their Maker! It was clearly the gulls' day, and Wayne and I felt extraneous; even invisible under their sky.

OCEAN CALENDAR

Who decides today what sea things come ashore?

I have witnessed olive shell, starfish, and sea anemone days. Today was clear jellyfish day, with the small, diamond-bright blobs strewn like mirrors along the sand. Another was horseshoe crab day. The beach was a junkyard of their helmets, and I stooped to examine one still wet from the wave that had tossed it downside up. The creature—part of whose scientific name is *limulus,* which aptly means "odd"—was still alive, but barely. More spider than crab, it weakly waved an appendage or two from the jumble of legs at its center, and I turned it over out of respect for its being and its dying.

One day was baby butterfly day. I have no idea what these tiny hinged shells the size of my fingernail are actually called, but when I saw them scattered like petals, I smiled to think no one else on the beach was taking note. Like miniature fritillaries, they were painted yellow, tan, pink, almond; some were even striped. What kind of world is this that a shell is a flower is a butterfly? Do I catch the Creator's eye when I say that word of recognition? Ahh!

WITHOUT THE CHERRY

What better way to spend a nor'easter than eating a banana split with your baby at the Silver Diner? That's what we're doing to escape the nerve-rattling wind—nothing like a cherry on top! Our waiter says he's hoping to be let out early, as his yard was already flooded when he left for work this morning. We hope he is too. We heard of one house that had washed into the sea. After paying the bill, we mount the big Ford pickup and ride homeward, high water splayed along each flank, my mind racing toward the black, huge sea ahead, the rising beyond all reason. From my safe seat I am free to imagine the ocean swallowing the boardwalk and tourist shops, the hotels, dance clubs, and pancake houses, to be glad the Atlantic trumps the Wilson for Senate sign and the corner Rite Aid. But what if the sea were coming for me?

TANGIER, VIRGINIA

1.

I fervently hope she will look up though I know she cannot see. She's dark-skinned and wears a bright pink shirt, and her black hair is decorated with feathery pink barrettes. She looks to be ten or eleven, and, though she's a big girl, she clings to her mother who carries her like a toddler, with head bowed. I guess she is from El Salvador or some such place and that she is adopted. A few moments before, I watched the captain help her down the ladder into the boat, carefully handing her as well as her white cane over to her mother, and now we are speeding across the bay, about twenty passengers in all, bound for Tangier.

Her mother and I exchange greetings, and I speak to her as well, but she frowns and shakes her head inside her mother's arms. As we leave the houses on the shore and enter open waters, I want her to look up and feel the sun on her face. How can such a child be coaxed into the light, I wonder. Glancing over a little later, I see she is standing up. Though her head remains bowed, glossy black hair hiding her face like a curtain, she allows her mother to extend her arms out into the spray.

I don't know how to measure love, but this arms-length reach into the wide, unknown world seems to me a hopeful span and an answer to my prayer on the way to Tangier.

2.

I follow the trail of the sanderling and leave my binoculars be-
hind. This way I won't be distracted by the need to name but
rather can allow the solitude of the beach to take me completely.
How good to be alone and feel alone, my mind awash with wings.
In distant pools where the bay has spilled itself I see bird shapes
rising and falling, hear calls and cries from a vague vista, a smear
of heaven behind the dunes.

3.

Tonight the town showed up, six snickering kids on the front
bench and everybody else in folding chairs that filled the museum.
I was screening our new documentary about the charity I work
for, Mercy Medical Airlift, which provides free "Angel Flights"
for patients when they need to go ashore for specialized medical
treatment. Tangier is prominently featured, with stunning aerial
shots and an interview with a Tangier resident named David and
the pilot, Dr. Neil Kaye, who flies him regularly for cancer treat-
ment in his red helicopter. Neil and his wife Susan, also a doctor,
have a second home on the island. Wayne and I are staying here,
at "Muddy Toes."

How many places in the U.S. can you go on a Friday night
and gather with the town folk to watch a movie advertised on
the street by word of mouth, where you pass the popcorn and
introduce yourself to people who are descendents of the original
settlers dating back to 1744 (though tradition has it that John
Crockett came with his family in 1686)—to people who talk in
a lilting brogue shaped into distinction, I'm told, from the origi-
nal Cornish dialect—who speak a somewhat "proper" version for
tourists, and another, more colorful tongue among themselves
called "talking backwards" where the opposite of what one means
is said. As Tangier native and linguist David Shores explains, one

might say, "It ain't rainin' none" when it's "raining pitchforks," or, "That's an easy lesson" when "it was an extremely difficult one."

Where but on Tangier do you hear people say "mommucked up" to describe a person badly injured, or "twee-wangled" for someone confused, or "crooked as an S-hook" for a liar. Where but Tangier can you find teenagers "cruising" in their golf carts on Friday nights and men who still follow the water for crabs, rising at 3 a.m. to launch their workboats and returning in late afternoon with their crab pots loaded? Though the island's eroding shores and declining population leave it vulnerable, its citizens maintain their distinctive identity.

At Spanky's several of us gather after the movie for ice cream and to share stories we've learned from the locals—legendary tales of storms and sons drowning, of church revivals and rivalries. Time on Tangier is old time. You see it in the hand-painted signs of shops with picket fences along narrow streets without cars, and in houses cozily planted side by side, some with a second front door allowing the waterman to slip out before dawn without waking his family. You hear it in the tuneful talk of neighbors who aren't in a hurry and in the raucous chorus of black skimmers on a shore undisturbed by development. True, the islanders have TV satellites, the Internet, and cell phones, but more community is found here than in the massive, faceless, modern islands of urban sprawl.

4.

After worshipping at Swain Memorial Methodist Church, we join the townsfolk for the annual Memorial Day service on the grounds adjacent to the crowded cemetery. A steady breeze blows off the encircling bay. The town is decked in the red, white, and blue of bunting and flags, streamers and lights, not to mention the occasional gentleman wearing an Old Glory necktie and the many ladies sporting red jackets with flag pins. Golf carts line the street, some embellished with signs like "Thank you" and "God Bless the USA."

The color guard marches in and Reverend Jones prays. Then Mr. Jack Thorne, a Navy veteran, tells of the fighting on Normandy Beach and the bodies on Okinawa, of how God Almighty protected him and everyone on the USS *Texas* save one sailor, and how, after the war and his return home, he celebrated the greatest Memorial Day of his life. That was when he answered an altar call issued by itinerant evangelist Oliver B. Greene and gave his life to Jesus, who was preparing for him a mansion in glory. He exhorts us to repent, giving it to us straight in the tradition of his God-fearing ancestors whose favorite hymn had these words: "The old ship of Zion is passing by. Will you list and go on board?" After he speaks, a slow quiet settles over the crowd, and seven girls in summer dresses line up before us, each holding a basket of rose petals.

The time has come for the reading of names, names spoken slowly and reverently—and for every name from every war, a toss of petals. Every Crockett, every Dise, every Evans, every Parks, every Pruitt—and others, too—Charnock, Harrison, Spence—beginning with World War I and continuing through the second war the litany of names spoken on an afternoon when children sit quietly and one man keeps saluting as names are read—name after name from Korea and Vietnam and at the last, from the Gulf war, with the breeze scattering the petals flung from the hands of the beautiful young daughters.

5.

Wayne and I walk on the beach the eve of our leave taking. He wants to photograph the sunset, and I want beach for beach's sake—all one and a half miles of unpeopled shore ending in a "fishhook" that looks distinctly like one on the map and holds a great deal of historical and religious history that I soaked up the whole time of our visit. We pass a forsaken crab pot or two, and tangleblown clusters of seaweed. We pass oystercatchers with long orange beaks and ospreys guarding their high, sprawling nests. To our right lies the Chesapeake, a name derived from the Algonquin word "Chesepiooc" which I'm told means "Great Shellfish Bay." The bay is two hundred miles long and thirty-five miles across at its widest point and was once sapphire blue, according to Captain John Smith, the English explorer who discovered Tangier Island in 1608. It is now more the color of tea as a result of the runoff pollution from over 16 million people living in the watershed. But on Tangier you feel removed from the contagion.

As I splash barefooted along the fringe, I think of Joshua Thomas, the legendary "parson of the islands," a waterman said to be of "natural roughness," who held Methodist-styled camp meetings on this very beach and in 1814 preached to some 12,000 British troops lined up in columns for words of exhortation before they sailed from Tangier for an attack on Baltimore. Recalling that day, Thomas said, "I never had such feelings in my life; but I felt determined to give them a faithful warning, even if those officers with their keen glittering swords would cut me in pieces for speaking the truth." He warned that "it was given me from the Almighty that they *could not* take Baltimore, and would *not succeed in their expedition.*" They did not succeed, and that is why we get to sing the Star Spangled Banner.

Wayne finds a good position from which to shoot the sunset—due to arrive, he estimates, in half an hour. I decide to walk to the end of the hook and hurry along as the light lessens until over my shoulder I can see Wayne no more, then make my way past a small region of grassy dunes as the tide is rising and the shore narrowing. Farther I walk on my solitary way with the bay washing over my feet and only a slim strip of sand remaining until

it vanishes into the darkening waters. Between me and the vast-
ness is a mere twelve inches of sand. I shudder to look at the rest
of my life and turn back toward the glow that was the sun.

2
TRIBUTARIES

SHENANDOAH DREAMS

The registration deadline is nearing for my high school reunion but I'm not going. I did the reunion thing once already and it wasn't fun. The cliques were still intact as if none of us were aging. The most intriguing part of that trip was passing through Front Royal on my way home and remembering Bowers Riverside Motor Court. I'd stopped at a Dairy Queen for ice cream and on a whim asked to see a phone book. Flipping through the yellow pages, my heart fluttered as I scanned the B's under Motels. No Bowers anywhere. I drove around a little, hoping instinct would take me to where the cabins—our cabin with red shutters—should be, by the banks of the Shenandoah. But this too was futile. It was getting late, so I got back on the road home.

I figured I'd try again some time. The place represents a certain wildness I've kept inside—silver river road, railroad tracks running alongside, banks of black-eyed Susans, cool cabin with pine walls, haunted trains shrilling through my dreams. How unlike the concrete maze of D.C., two hours east, which I remember as a riddle of school and schedules and knotted nerves my stepfather complained of as he struggled with traffic, work, and the task of fathering three new daughters, Robyn, Leslie, and Suzy.

Once in a while, in the summer, we would load up our chrome-heavy, commodious Buick Special, roll down the windows, and drive to Front Royal along State Route 55. City gray would gradually blur to green. This I absorbed with my whole face. Daddy challenged us to a game of "Zip," where a cow earned you two points, a horse five, and a windmill a whopping twenty—provided you were the first to say zip. The comic book in my lap remained closed as the ride went on, with telephone poles racing by and the wind roaring and the air cacophonous with our voices.

Finally, we arrived in Front Royal, met at the junction by a man sitting outside in a chair. He jumped up to greet our car and hand us a brochure advertising the world-famous Caverns of Luray (more famous, no doubt, than the rival Dixie Caverns). Through traffic and heat we drove up and around for a while, until trees grew darkly on both sides of the road. Suddenly the sign came into view for Bowers' Riverside Motor Court, and we were pulling into the driveway and there was Mr. Bowers coming out of the office in his plaid shirt, grinning as he gave us the key to number three, the biggest and best cabin. It was white stucco with red shutters and came with a backyard cow that I befriended and named Bossie. Our bedroom had the most delicious cold-mountain smell, and the sheets were crisp as day-old snow. After choosing beds, my sisters and I would light out for the river, sliding down the bank, pulling off shoes to wade in the shocking water. The smooth stones felt like the soles of our own bare feet. Once, when the river was low, we kept our sneakers on and sloshed all up and down and across to a pasture, pretending to be escaped slaves.

The other famous adventure was walking along the railroad tracks, sometimes for miles. On one side was a mountain face and an occasional cave. On the other was the Shenandoah.

Rock and river: a perfect picture, so now it seems, of a child's life of form and freedom. Sometimes we would see skeletons of small animals or pick up railroad spikes for souvenirs, or put a penny on the track in case a train came by. But mostly I marveled at the gleaming rails going on forever in this wild, lonely region of dragonflies and surging weeds and bones at my feet.

Our stepfather was a fine-featured man with reddish hair and sensitive brown eyes, who married my mother when I was five. He was an artist and worked for the government, an odd pairing indeed. Both he and Mom had suffered through bad marriages. Children perplexed him and he was easily irritated by loud voices, arguing, and accidents of any sort. At home in Arlington, we lived under strict discipline. But during family outings, Daddy relaxed; he laughed and teased and tickled grandly, loosening up in the shade of Mr. Bowers' maple trees, teaching us to skip rocks and play "washers," a game of his own. It was like horseshoes, only played by pitching a washer with hopes of leaning or landing it in a hole.

At night we played Texas 42 in the kitchen. Competition was furious and hilarious. The dominoes clicked as we shuffled them on the table and bid outrageously on dubious hands, counting on our partners to come through. Being on Daddy's team usually assured victory.

One night he made chili, another Texas specialty. (He was born in Weatherford, "the watermelon capital of the world," he would brag, though I've since learned that quite a few other towns make the same claim.) My sisters and I set the table, a sturdy maple rectangle covered with a flowered oilcloth that concealed a slight unevenness between leaves that often spilled our milk. From time to time Daddy appeared to add spices or stir. At last it was ready. Mom brought the salad and we sat down. The blessing was said; we began to eat. One by one our faces registered surprise. Too hot, said our mother. Daddy added sugar. We ate again, then grimaced. Too sweet. Daddy added water, stirred things around, then poured in salt. This too was ruinous. The chili was dumped and we ate sandwiches that night. I've often thought this incident captured the essence of my stepfather's awkwardness at loving.

The last time we went to Riverside Motor Court, I was thirteen and knew for sure I'd been given a seeing eye. That is why I sat alone on the river bank the morning we were leaving, studying the smooth-running water, the Susan flowers bearing my name, the high-floating clouds. I told the Shenandoah it was my river and sang its song. Even now, hiking at middle age, I like to drop back from the group to shut my eyes and see the spearing cries of crows or walls of wind buckling over ridges.

Where are John Bowers' cabins? By the river, where they belong.

MR. BOH AND BELA

I recently acquired an unusual memento from my mother's estate that brought me in touch with a good side of my stepfather—his pleasure in seeing me and my sisters scared out of our wits.

The object is a National Bohemian beer goblet, a thick glass bearing the face and swooping black mustache of Mr. Boh, the company's mascot, and the words, "Oh boy, what a beer!" It wasn't beer that Daddy put in our glasses, but grape soda and scoops of vanilla ice cream. This sweetness was the accompaniment to a midnight viewing of *Dracula* and another unforgettable face.

On condition that we were in bed promptly by seven, we were invited to the movie, and in the midnight hour, awakened by Daddy's knock on the door. Downstairs, we took our seats in the dark while he prepared the floats, then turned out the only light in the house. He made his way into the living room singing "oooh-oooh-oooh" in the likeness of a ghost ascending and descending stairs. Then he switched on his hero, Bela Lugosi.

The signature cape, nobleman's air, blazing eyes, beckoning hand—and his voice with its slow, heavy accent and hypnotic intonations—the totality of these images bored into my mind like a terrifying worm, even as the white, beautiful throats of ladies in filmy gowns were savaged under cover of Dracula's cloak. Only the crucifix with its power to arrest the fiend could relieve my horror. Afterward, I lay in bed awake for hours, my mind seared by the turning wheel of images.

And yet I thought the dark party a happy affair, to violate my bedtime and sit beside my sisters on the couch with my ice cream float as Daddy relished Bela's horror and its effects on us—a strange way indeed to forge a fatherhood.

HOUSE ON HATEMONGER HILL

George Lincoln Rockwell and his storm troopers were the terror of Dominion Hills and a thrill to us teenagers who hung out at Brenner's Malt Shop. One afternoon we found our blood running wonderfully cold when Rockwell's men in trench coats sat close by. What could be better than having real Nazis in the booth right behind you? And yet we were sickened when one of their pamphlets surfaced with the words, "Ship the Niggers Back to Africa."

I was about fourteen when the American Nazi Party established its headquarters in a secluded, crumbling farmhouse across Wilson Boulevard, a road two blocks from my house. It was surrounded with barbed wire and guarded by a Doberman, and some boys I knew once tried to sneak onto the grounds to spy but were shot with salt pellets and got out of there fast. Apparently, as I later learned, Rockwell chose my neighborhood because it was the place of "white flight" from the District of Columbia, and the Nazis imagined they would find sympathy with my neighbors. Sadly, they did with some, but those neighbors didn't wear Swastikas.

A few years before, someone had written "nigger" in chalk on the sidewalk in front of our house. My parents said it was because of Hazel, our black-skinned sitter, who rode the bus from Washington and seemed, with her rich humor and ample lap, to be as much a part of our family as any relative. It hurt me to think of someone calling her a bad name.

Then there was the man who knocked on our door and warned my stepfather that "these aren't the kind of people we allow here in our neighborhood." He was referring to the jazz artists who came as guests to our house. Daddy was friends with many musicians—Louis Armstrong, trombonist Trummy Young, violinist Stuff Smith, to name a few. I remember jam sessions in the basement with lots of people and hot jazz music and dancing and getting to meet many famous artists, whom Daddy drew as remarkable pen and ink portraits to hang on his studio wall after obtaining the prized autographs.

To the rude man who knocked on our door, he said, "I don't tell you who you can invite to your house, and you don't tell me who I can invite to mine."

The summer Rockwell was assassinated I was sixteen and away with my friend and neighbor, Linda, on Mackinac Island, Michigan, where we worked as cooks for a wealthy woman named Mrs. Erwin at her summer home on a cliff overlooking Lake Huron. Word quickly reached us that Rockwell had been gunned down by a former party member outside the laundromat next door to our malt shop; that my sister Robyn's boyfriend heard the shots; that my sister, Leslie, saw the draped corpse and blood on the pavement; and that Linda's dog Charlie became famous for chomping the backside of the assassin as he ran through Linda's yard in his frantic escape. A few hours later, John Patler was arrested while waiting at a bus stop. To think I missed it all!

THE THIRD DAY OF SPRING

The spring of my sister Robyn's death I became aware that under the floor I walked on was an abyss. All the surfaces of the house—countertops, table, lampshades, rocking chair—were bounded by a devouring deadness. It would sometimes awaken me at night and I would sit straight up in bed. In the backyard, forsythia blazed, doves nested, but I wandered about benumbed. It was the same when my stepfather lay in a coma and I planted onions in March in a frozen garden. The dirt, the cold, the bulbs anchored me to the world when inside all was lost and I feared the Infinite spaces.

The dead thing I remember from childhood is Petey, our beloved blue parakeet. He died in Robyn's hands at the ripe age of twelve. We put him in a cardboard box and tearfully buried him in "the jungle," the unkempt, sunken part of our yard. Days passed. I wondered about him who had played the clown atop my head, babbling with glee. I remembered how he would fly to the bedroom mirror to adore the other laughing bird and how, when the lights were off and my sisters and I in bed, he would sing in a burbling murmur under his cage cover until ebbing off to sleep. Such a small creature to bring so much joy through our family's divides. When I noticed a cat passing through the yard, I decided this was reason enough to check on Petey, so I dug up the box and opened it. There he was as before, but even more dead, his claws curled up, his eyes sealed. I had believed for an empty box.

Today is the third day of spring; tomorrow, Easter. This new green world shivers in the sun's pure wash. It is a universe away from that other blank world. I think of Jesus slipping in agony through the crack of space into formless horror. No one else has seen the whole. It swallowed him, a bleeding, writhing disgrace, but only for a flicker of time, for he swam out of that obscene belly and reversed death. That is why whoever comes to him finds shelter. He sees the heart's abyss and hurls himself in, thorny head first, all the way to hell. No one need stand shaking in the cold.

SCRAPBOOK PAGES

It started with a scrapbook. I began creating it as a birthday gift for my niece, Cynthia—one of those artsy-craftsy books that are an industry in their own right, occupying entire aisles in the big craft stores, with an infinite variety of colored and patterned papers and stick-on embellishments and tags on which to write "journal" entries. The subject is my mother, Mary Lee, Cynthia's grandmother.

The project took on a life of its own and indeed, seemed to have power to summon the enormous, slumberous past, for as I cut checkered papers with scalloping scissors and pasted down neon letters, beach umbrellas, and dragonflies to enhance the dozens of photographs selected from boxes and manila envelopes recovered from my mother's estate—as I brought the pages to life displaying Mary Lee eating wedding cake with my father, or lounging in a swimsuit with her long, shapely legs, or standing in front of our house with us, her three daughters in organdy Easter dresses, or posing with jazz drummer Gene Krupa, or holding my infant niece and gazing raptly into the rosebud face, or kissing John, her third husband, or grinning mischievously that last sad month with her cancer wig askew, or any of the other windows on her life that would tell her vibrant story—these pages designed over a few weeks' time seemed magically to set in motion a series of reunions that reconciled the past with my present, stirring within me a joyous and unexpected sense of wholeness.

. . .

The first is a visit with my girlhood friend Linda in my old neighborhood on Ninth Street North. After her parents died, she bought out her brothers' interests in the home of their childhood and moved back in. So now it is years later and we are looking at each other with wonder in her two-story brick house right across the street from where I grew up. All the houses in Dominion Hills were built right after World War II and are identical except for different colors of shutters and doors. We sit in her living room that is the living room we hurried through as girls, bypassing the boring, seated adults as we were on our way to some sort of excitement. It is the identical room except for different furniture and rugs and the fact that she and I are weightier and somewhat wiser than before as we laugh about the ice cube, cork, and darning needle she used to pierce my ears and many other girls' too. We remember how, when the Twist became the rage, we spun Chubby Checker on her record player and danced wildly in her basement, the feverish motions seeming to churn the future into any fantastic shape we could conceive; or the summer her dog became a celebrity for chasing and biting Rockwell's assassin as he raced through Linda's yard—when summer evenings were filled with lightning bugs and loud kids playing dodge ball in the street; when the grown-ups referred to each other as Mrs. Burgess or Mrs. Eslinger, and there was Mrs. Murza from Lithuania whose house smelled like cabbage and who would babysit my sisters and me and call us "zhe girlies." Those were the days of Civil Defense drills in school when the class had to get down on elbows and knees, one in front of the other, and I noted the large unpleasantness of Andrew Timetheo's rear end, and how on another day I walked home from school with lead in my stomach fearing we would all be blown up by a missile aimed at us from Cuba.

But now the time has come to leave Linda and Ninth Street, with promises to stay in touch and see each other again soon. Wayne and I drive to Clyde's, a restaurant in northern Virginia where after over thirty years of separation, I am to meet my best friends from college. They're in town with some of our other close friends for their high school reunion, and we've arranged to have brunch together.

I am trying to understand what I mean by "best friends." Obviously, it is the draw of common interests, shared experience, the phase of life one is in, and where one is in the world. In the case of the friends I would soon be seeing, we were girls of a golden time, responsible for no one but ourselves, viewing the world and its possibilities with exuberance. Our friendships emerged from the tabula rasa of the freshman life, the fresh start, the boat everyone was in. What we were before, where we lived, and what our families were like was inconsequential. Now was the time to seize the day. Our school was Madison College, an all-women's state teachers' college—at least for the first two years when we had to sign in and out for dates and observe a curfew and answer to a housemother. Then everything changed and a men's dorm was built and we could come and go as we pleased and wear slacks to class, and one spring night we watched the National Guard rumble down our small-town campus streets to quell an anti-war demonstration that had somehow exploded out of a water fight.

I met Bonnie and Ginny during a hall meeting designed to lay down the rules and routines of dorm life. They invited me afterward to visit in their room. My own roommates were Lynn and Mary Lou, the first being a big-boned upperclassman majoring in P. E. who had claimed the best of everything, leaving me and Mary Lou, a shy and devout Catholic with red hair and freckles, with the bunk beds and shared dresser. Lynn favored falling asleep to the sounds of the Lettermen, which not even my pillow pressed against one ear could shut out, so that I wound up going to the college nurse for sleeping pills—but the second semester, my lot improved and I moved down the hall to share a suite with my new friends. Bonnie was blond, insouciant, outgoing, and fun-loving; Ginny was brown-haired, practical, loyal, and quick to speak her mind. I was both serious and spontaneous, and the three of us seemed to complement each other perfectly. We held all things in common—clothes and make-up, all-nighters, exam anxiety, parties, music, tears—the highs and lows of a fast-flowing time, the interwoven cords that would last despite decades of eventful separation.

Wayne and I arrive at Clyde's early and wait at an outdoor table for the moment I've dreamed of for years—to see those faces! The minutes hang maddeningly in the air like steam from our coffee cups. How to sit still as I am about to meet the women last seen saying tearful goodbyes when the doors of our cars slammed shut and we drove off loaded with four years of social and intellectual growth stuffed into boxes as books and more books and papers with hard-won grades; coffee mugs, sorority pins, dried flowers and photographs, all signifying our studies, friendships, and heartthrobs that would help to shape our separate destinies.

Two cars pull into the parking lot and Bonnie and Ginny emerge—stylish and smiling—as well as other dear friends from college days—Les, Mary, Leigh. We hug. I cry. We find a table and exchange stories, memories, pictures—entire histories squeezed into two hours—careers, marriages, children, grandchildren, the death of parents. Strangely, it seems we are exactly as we were before, only more so, each beautiful and young despite the creases in our faces, unchanged by the gravity of intervening years and blows. And then it's time to leave, to hug goodbye and return to

Texas, New Jersey, Arizona, Virginia—to resume the ebbing and flowing lives that have been given to us—with plans to meet a year or so from now.

· · ·

There is still another reunion, an astonishing scrapbook page springing from a mouse click. On impulse, I Google my father's name and land on an obituary. A child's dark, smiling eyes look up at me, the eyes of one twelve-year-old Zachary who died four days after a tragic zip-line accident at a church retreat. His grandparents—to my astonishment—are my father and his wife. His mother is Sally. *Sally.* This would be my unknown half sister, one of three half siblings who have existed only as names in my mind but who, for their entire lives, have inhabited my father's hemisphere, the part that was lost to me at age four when he ended the marriage to my mother. I am both sad and joyful as I follow more leads—a foundation created in Zach's honor with the motto, "Serving to Change Lives for Eternity." An email address for Sally.

I write to her, identifying myself as—unlikely as it seems—her half-sister, Suzanne. Soon she writes back. We exchange phone numbers and agree to talk one afternoon. We talk for hours. So many fragments of time and place still to be accounted for—Idaho, Monterey, Christmas 1953, New York, D.C.—what and when and why? A picture of a wedding party offering toasts. A sepia photo of tents in Tripoli. A memory of my father walking away, wearing a jacket, not looking back.

Brooding on these mysteries, I walk on the beach today scouting for sea glass. The expanse of water and shore brings my lost nephew to mind. In the YouTube clips following his untimely death, in the blogs and newspaper articles, his love for God resounds. Such a young man to have such serious faith! He had wanted to be a professional baseball player and give his money to the poor. This came after a trip to an orphanage in Jamaica where he hugged the children flocking around him and told his parents he wanted to adopt them. Now his dreams lead others on. As a project of the Z Foundation, his parents took a team of volunteers to Jamaica and built a playground at the orphanage. At home in Tennessee, they organized volunteers to work in an inner city housing project and minister to families by serving holiday dinners and playing games with children in the Boys and Girls Clubs.

So much good has come from tragedy—remnants of my life coming together, pieces of joy coming into the lives of children. Picking sea glass from among the shells makes me think that maybe Zach sees from eternity all fragments rejoined to their rightful bottles.

THE HEART HAS ITS HUNGER

The heart has its hunger but God is the one who names the day of fulfillment.

I am looking back at a paper-doll chain of my former selves, remembering the child who built a flower altar to God in the back yard; the night of fever when I reached out my believing arm to Jesus and begged him to appear and take my hand until my arm ached and I saw he wasn't coming; the visit to an empty chapel where I felt God's presence and wanted to belong to him and him alone.

Years later, I finally yielded to a co-worker's repeated invitations to attend her church and sat in the balcony watching a choir of deaf mutes sing hymns through their hands and found myself in tears, which only increased as the Pentecostal preacher gave an altar call and said he *knew* there was someone in the church who needed to come down and accept the Lord. Confused and embarrassed, I hurried out.

Another time, when I was a graduate student, I found myself staring at a sign on the bulletin board in my apartment lobby with the words, "Seeking Christian fellowship? Come up to 5-L." What in the world was Christian fellowship? I didn't know, but I wanted it. I looked at that sign a dozen times before finally mustering the courage to take the elevator up.

I had foreseen how it would be when I knocked on the door—there would be a warm welcome with loving hugs, and I would be safe among the Christians and could release the great pressure I felt inside, the ache that went with me everywhere—to my classes, to parties, the library, the psychiatrist, the store for beer and cigarettes, the long drives in the countryside to escape the burning unease. There I stood at 5-L and heard music behind the door, some sort of Christian recording, and I began to think, "This is sort of hokey. This is really quite simplistic." The thought grew, diminishing the girls on the other side with their artless faith as I realized I was too refined for this music—too smart for the childish Christian thing, and I turned back with relief and burning.

There *was* one certainty I held that stayed constant—that God had to be someone who understood suffering. I loathed soft theology and all notions of God as a big, wish-granting teddy bear. In "Raggedy Ann on God" and with the myth of Icarus in mind, I wrote (you can tell it was the 70s),

> O God, who art a pushover,
> loves rubber babies
> and any clay-soft,
> tit-adoring thing:
> Why have you forsaken me?
> Is it my arrowbones?
> The scars I see with?
>
> Go on, honky, try me.
>
> Stick your son like a gun in my ribs.
> It's flesh you smell, not wax,
> and believe me, daddy,
> these wings are no prayers.

I will claw your dimpled hands
and rake your eyes,
and twist that plushy image
like a dove's neck.
I will not have you amused
and babbling with your play-doh:

I'm shaped too like a cross to let you off so easy.

I met him on his bloody cross in Delmas Jones' Sunday school class in Memphis, Tennessee. I had moved there after completing my graduate program to live with my sister, Robyn, and her family, and out of a desire to be spiritual, was attending her church, though secretly I ridiculed the Southern accents and corny hymns, the stories of angels, Noah's ark, Jonah and the whale.

Delmas had been to the holy land. He had seen the huge thorns of the sort that were woven into the crown pressed into Christ's head, and the heavy whip with its balls of lead to tear the flesh. He described the iron nails driven into the wrists and feet, and the excruciating pain as the bleeding Christ heaved to push upward to breathe. In that tableau of horror, I saw his woeful face looking straight at me.

3
CHANNELS

WONDERFUL HAND

My son brought home an amazing machine he'd found in the sand. He demonstrated its variable motions—a pincer claw made for grasping, and jointed segments allowing the arm to pivot and its "elbow" to bend. He said the crab's small robotic arm was wondrous, and I immediately thought of Dr. Mahler.

Dr. Andrew Mahler was an impressively large and kindly older man who taught upper level literature classes when I was in college. He had white, thinning hair and wore a suit as was proper for English professors then, just as it was proper for me to be called Miss Underwood. I was furiously taking notes as he named the characteristics of the Romantic era—a fascination with the long-ago and far-away, and a preference for the common man and individualism as opposed to the aristocracy and social conventions enthroned by the Neo-Classicists. The gardens of those Romantics were riotous, their religion pantheistic, and their temperament rebellious. They were lovers of nature. They had a sense of wonder . . . I was poised to keep writing, but then noticed Dr. Mahler had stopped talking. He stood before us with his arm extended and his hand—a big, knobby, spotted hand—slowly began squeezing open and shut. He explained that he had suffered a stroke a few years ago and couldn't move on one whole side of his body but that he had thankfully regained his mobility and came to see what a miracle his hand was. "That," he said, opening and shutting his hand like a burgeoning flower, "is wonder full."

I also thought of how Jean Paul Sartre had discovered the wonder of the hand before he died. His words to his friend Peter Victor are not those of the atheist he had been throughout his life, but those of a believer: "I do not feel that I am the product of chance, a speck of dust in the universe, but someone who was expected, prepared, prefigured. In short, a being whom only a Creator could put here; and this idea of a creating hand refers to God."

AUNT CLAIRE

Bathing her, I feigned nonchalance. My neighbor, Claire Evelyn, was suddenly old and needing to lean. I filled the sink and washed her face and torso with its single breast and the white scar where the other had been, and she washed the rest. We finished off with a dusting of floral-scented powder that restored a bit of class, masking the rawness and glare. She needed me to select her blouse and slacks for the day and brush white hairs from her pillow and help ease her trembling form into her chair. I could not fail her now, for she had been my friend for many years and was "Aunt Claire" to my family. She was a schoolteacher from a well-mannered age who had always borne herself like a Greek column, had given piano lessons to my three children and attempted the same with me, and sometimes could be heard singing from inside her house, the balmy air of a summer evening carrying her strong soprano notes into the street.

She came from the era of women's clubs and belonged to several. I went with her to Study Club in a home of brocade drapes and mauve carpet. We, the ladies, held bone china cups on our laps and drank coffee poured from a silver pot and ate lemon cake as the Collect was read. They were a welcoming group with smoothly coiffed hair and diamonds on their blue-veined hands, smiling to have a younger woman among them, one who held it as marvelous that the club went elegantly on, even as it was reported that this or that member had suffered a stroke or taken a bad fall—even as the ladies were leaving one by one with none to take their places.

The mornings I cared for her, Claire Evelyn liked for me to make muffins and tea and to sit with her in the den with its gold-painted walls and cabinet of collectible dolls for all seasons. On those mornings we were saying to lupus and cancer and all the ills that ravage the body, "We are, after all, human beings, and we will enjoy our tea."

WATERMARKS

A boy I'll call Ron once overheard his mother telling a friend, "I wish it had been Ron who died, not Billy." Billy was Ron's little brother who had died in infancy. The cruel words continued to cut inside throughout his life, and he too became cruel. He was a caricaturist by profession and knew how to size a person up. With a few pen strokes he exposed and exaggerated the shameful flaw, making it definitive. He didn't need a pen, though, to label his subjects, which he did routinely at dinner. He made known to his family all the people in his office by their big noses and bald spots, by their ignorance or cowardice. It was an uncanny ability, this seizing on weakness, and his wife and children were duly characterized. Not even the neighbors got off the hook: fruitcakes, phonies, and liars lived in the houses up and down the street. That was years before the family found healing in the knowledge that God's love translates the flaws, the scars, into beautiful watermarks.

HER GRANDMOTHER
LILLIAN'S GOWN

My friend invited me for tea and to show me a patch square as
Kansas pieced to the upper left back of her Grandmother Lillian's
nightgown. She'd found it in an old steamer trunk in the Fort
Scott family home among clothes that fell apart like cobwebs. She
set the gown to soaking in bleach water and aired it in the sun to
hang like a happy soul on the line, its whiteness come back and
the threads still strong. "This patch is like one of *my* patches," Sara
said. "I try to make things last."

She showed me Lillian's portrait hanging on the upstairs wall,
a young woman with pale Dutch braids and level blue eyes match-
ing her own. She told me Lillian had died in childbirth—while
giving birth to *her* mother—and presented me with a snapshot
of that beautiful, grown-up mother laughing too loudly at the
captain's party. Throughout childhood, it had been Sara's job to
manage the house and her seldom straight mother.

She confided that she'd worn the gown to bed the night be-
fore as if to slip into the skin of the grandmother she'd never
known but whose sturdy mending was a clue to her selfsame
resourcefulness. I imagined her waking that morning in the old-
fashioned gown with its gussets and buttons intact, more truly
herself in the flow of lasting white, more certain of the future as
we all are when we find our strongest thread.

NO MORE RABBITS

He gave signs, but they were not properly read. His family and friends sympathized with his failures and tried to help him, sending a little money or inviting him for Christmas. It wasn't enough. He had become obese and suffered from health problems. He walked with great difficulty. He had lost his job. He faced eviction. He was gay. He was alone.

I knew him as a little boy, him and his twin brother. Who would have foreseen that the smiling child with freckles and glasses visiting his cousin Linda in her house across the street from mine would wake up very early one morning and heave himself into his car, drive down vacant streets leading to the university where he had worked, place his keys on the front seat, struggle to reach his building and the iron steps of the fire escape he climbed one by one, pushing his legs upward toward roof and sky, forcing his body to execute the plan he had mentally rehearsed for months—perhaps years—on days when the campus was a throbbing hive of students and teachers hurrying on their way, the mingled voices, the colored sweaters and wavering trees, doors opening and closing, his heart wildly beating as he pitched himself up and up the iron stairs to the roof and balanced himself in silence—drawing together the dissipated parts of his mind and heart and all his blind choices that led to this moment as he hovered on the edge before jumping, drawing down with him the faces of those who had jeered, ignored, or pushed away, including at the last, his own unfathomable face? He was found later that morning, a broken, bleeding puzzle.

I thought of him the other day when my friend told me he had no more rabbits to pull out of his hat. He'd lost his job and girlfriend. His despair frightened me. I know it well, for I too have been on the edge. I mentioned Jesus. He doesn't believe. Still, I can pray. Like a foolish root in a concrete slab, I hope my prayer will grow and wind upward and crack open the impossible riddle of life without God.

JOHNNY

He used to call from the road. I'd ask, "Where are you?"

He'd say, "Heck, I don't know." He would be in Albany or Chicago or Nashville. "Do you have a minute to listen to a song?" From some faraway mountain or sleeping city, he'd sing his new lines for me: "Behind the veil, hearts may be breaking" or "Life seems like just a dream where the rivers ebb and flow . . ."

He was Johnny Reid, and he was my friend. He had a big frame and a raw-boned voice with a Tidewater accent. He was a truck driver possessing an artist's soul. He loved his wife Sherry and they laughed a lot together. Through her, he found faith in Christ and was delivered of powerful addictions. He was a passionate reader and listened to audio books on the road—especially biographies. His religion was thoughtful and deep, and he feared not to ask questions. He cried openly. He cared for people. Every conversation he ended saying, "Let's have a word of prayer."

When he was home in Virginia Beach, he'd sometimes drop by the Angel Flight office to join us before work for devotions. We were always pleased when he'd bring his guitar and sing his latest song. Afterwards he'd stop by my desk, and we'd talk about our families, our spiritual struggles, our artistic journeys. When I would ask about his song-writing career, his answers were either way high or depressingly down. He had received backing to produce a recording of his best work, performed by professional vocalists and Nashville musicians. It was a complicated and drawn-out process, but finally the strands came together.

As soon as he obtained the master copy, he drove over to my office and invited me to listen. I'll never forget the sweltering summer morning sitting in his black Mustang with the engine running and the air conditioner wheezing as he played the new-minted master and we listened with elation and tears to the songs forged over lonely highways, songs with titles like "Cross beside the Road," "Sacred Mountain," "Where the Crimson River Flows." The rich blending of voices with mandolins and fiddles or a bluesy piano delivered the down-home lyrics with power and inevitability. With that recording, he signed on with a major music company and acquired an agent. One of his songs ranked on a Southern Gospel chart.

But he never quite made it. The alternation of blinding hope and grievous rejection took its toll. That, and being laid off. That, and having a heart condition. The last time I saw Johnny, he was in the hospital, propped up in bed with a biography of John Adams beside him. Sherry was with him, and despite his drawn, pallid face and shortness of breath, he joked and put us at ease. He gave me a folded piece of paper and asked me to type up something he'd written and if I would read it for devotions at Angel Flight. Of course, I told him, and the next day I did, though it was hard to get through it. *The heart longs for home, it's a given fact. Although we don't normally dwell on the thought, deep in the heart's recesses, the longing is always there. We build temporary shelters with touches of nostalgia. We put into these dwellings remnants of our past and hopes for our future. We touch up here and tear down there, but in our more lucid moments, we realize that it just doesn't measure up to what we remember as home.*

And then he died, as if to answer the yearning expressed in his last written words:

If home is where the heart is—your home and mine—if we have given our heart to Jesus, that is where Jesus is. You see, this is where we are loved and cared for, where we are accepted just as we are, where tears are wiped away and fears are put to rest. Home is love in the purest sense. I have come to know and believe the love God has for us. For God is love, and whoever dwells (or makes his home in him) is love, and he or she dwells in God and God dwells in him.

Sometimes I just can't wait to go home.

O. D. AND RUTH

In a flat West Texas land of cotton and cattle egrets, O. D. and Ruth Rhodes go about their day. It's a day that lives in my mind as a pastiche of images drawn from old family movies, photographs, and stories recounted over dinner with my husband or during one of the Rhodes' family reunions. On this day, O. D.—short for Oren Dee—drives his Chevy pickup to the town of Petersburg to talk business with his son Harold Dee, who manages his implement dealership. If you had ridden with him that morning on the farm-to-market road and looked back over your shoulder, you would have seen the words "O. D. Rhodes' Farm" painted in huge black letters on the barn. O. D. bought land right before the Great Depression for $20 an acre and irrigated his crops of cotton, maize, and alfalfa with enough success to pay his bank mortgage. Over time, he thrived and built his family a fine house in a grove of shade trees.

A big, handsome man with a shock of dark hair, he's known in the community for his upright character, though not so upright that he doesn't get a charge out of racing his friend to church on Sunday mornings. But so upright that once when he came to blows with an ornery neighbor over a property dispute, he drove twenty-seven miles to the county seat and turned himself in for breaking the law against fighting. Dutifully, he paid the fine.

This afternoon as the heat grows and business slacks off, he and his friends will play Texas 42 in the back of his shop and discuss weather and the price of cotton.

On this same day, Ruth drives to town, too, in her Buick sedan. She has her own floral shop and many orders to fill. She and her daughter Orene went to school in Kansas City for several months to learn flowers. Despite her husband's objections, she's wearing a polyester pantsuit. Like him, she's the subject of family legends, having given birth to eight children and survived the loss of three. How deep her hurt must be, but who would know, for in her dignity she maintains a level presence.

A story will be told years later of how when she is seventy-eight and driving home late at night after visiting friends, she makes a wrong turn and ends up on a road flooded by a spreading lake. As her efforts to drive out of the water fail, she exits the car and starts walking. To guide herself in the pitch black dark and waist-deep water, she follows a barbed wire fence with her hand that eventually leads around the lake to dry pavement. At this point, Ruth is exhausted, bleeding, and cold, for the temperature is near freezing. She lies down to spend the night on the road, to be found the next day by a farmer and taken home, blessedly sound in body and mind.

Merging into this picture is an image of Wayne, their young-est son, born when Ruth was in her early forties. O. D. calls him Shorty. Wayne is seven or eight and riding a motorbike to visit his older brother Skeet, forty miles away. Or, he's spending the night with his buddies on a raft in the cow pasture pond, or grabbing a rifle by the back door to hunt jackrabbits, or lying in a hay-warm stall beside his prize Chester White sow and her new litter at the county fair. He tells me his parents never questioned his coming and going nor worried about snakes or storms. He also remembers never hearing them raise their voices. Though outward displays of affection were seldom apparent, Wayne never doubted that he was loved and that he was free to pursue any dream he fancied. More than in the black and white photos and grainy films formatted on DVD, Ruth and O. D. live for me in the calm eyes that quiet me or the adventurous eyes that follow me across the room.

ALL THAT JAZZ

Oh, how her red hair enflamed him. That's what he said started their romance. They were both widowed. She was seventy-seven; he, eighty-four. She was a jazz writer, he a jazz musician. She lived in North and he in South Carolina. One fall day he telephoned and said, "Do you want to look at leaves?" She said yes. A photograph from their first date shows them on an overlook on the Blue Ridge Parkway with the mountains all ablaze and her short, curly hair the same reddish gold as the leaves. He has his arm around her, and they are both smiling like gleeful children.

The next thing I knew, he'd proposed, and the wedding date was set for June. But as the day drew near, she balked. How was she going to leave her daughter, Leslie, and her grand and great grandchildren? How to leave the cool, green town of Asheville that had been her home for fifteen years, ever since she'd left Memphis and the grave of her oldest daughter, Robyn? Or leave the church she loved with its contemporary praise and worship that stirred in her a fresh excitement about God. She needed time. John Haynes was patient. He waited. She confirmed.

On August 30, 2003, my mother became Mary Lee Haynes. Her pastor, Steve, conducted the ceremony and made no bones of his delight in uniting the most senior couple of his ministry. They were an elegant pair, she in her flowing blue dress with a bouquet of red roses in her hand; he with snow-white hair, dark suit, boutonniere. Afterward, they fed each other cake and carried on as lovebirds do.

It was to be a short-lived marriage of only three and a half years, but what fun those years held. They honeymooned in Charleston, drove to Horseshoe, Texas, and back, took trips to the beach, and attended jazz festivals where John, who'd had his own band for many years, played his bass fiddle. Mary Lee enjoyed her own fame among the fans, for she'd written a book, *Going to Kansas City,* and wrote articles regularly for the *Mississippi Rag,* both jazz publications. Their romance was the subject of a local newspaper article and quoted John as saying, "She and I are old enough to have heard all the songs they have written for the last seventy-five years. We ride down the road and sing all the songs, and for ones we don't know, we hum."

It was lovely music that no one wanted to end. But lung cancer stopped it. John saw her through brutal days of chemo and radiation, begged her, scolded her for refusing to drink water or eat even a bite or two of food. In the end, when she was brought home from the hospital and placed under hospice care, he played his guitar and tenderly sang the songs and hymns she loved, singing all night until she could no longer hear.

4
TIDEPOOLS

THE SOUL'S BLOOD

Church-bels beyond the stars heard, the souls bloud,
The land of spices, something understood.
——George Herbert, *Prayer (I)*

A pheasant disappearing into the brush is how Wallace Stevens defines poetry, alluding to the almost-not quite nature of flaming words that tantalize and invite us to a place we cannot go—not through the square hole of logic, that is. But through the vortex of imagination we can follow the pheasant and lo, be fellow pheasant.

Prayer is pheasant-like. It is good to think of this when I find myself squaring words to a God I believe in propositionally. *This day. You must. I want. Lead not.* All the while, the deep, aching tremors of the Spirit rise like a buried sea to carry my flotsam words, pitching them on the far shore where God is walking this day. He reaches down and plucks them from the sand, bright gems that represent depths of grief and love behind the words, the flat, failed words.

On other days I catch him by the hem and he turns to see. With this prayer, I want for nothing. I follow him into silence that lives and breathes, and we are one: heart, kernel, marrow. Prayer is an embryo: unspoken, understood.

BROKEN TEETH

I affirm to my dentist I no longer clench my teeth and need not wear my orthotic during the day. But she finds more broken teeth and says they have to be extracted and that I will need implants and crowns to replace cracked crowns, and that I should be glad it's only my teeth and not my heart.

I think it is my heart. If I am blind to so costly and destructive a habit as teeth-grinding, how blind am I to other flaws? I've been reading a book about the classical Christian disciplines of prayer, study, service, etc.—and despite the author's insistence on grace, not legalism, his mirror shows ugly flaws: pettiness, complacency, unbelief.

His dark glass is particularly unsettling because I've always considered the habit of self-abasement to be grotesque, not to mention insincere. Puritans with their endless groveling before God, the most extreme example being that of the neurotic Reverend Michael Wigglesworth, author of the sulfurous poem *Day of Doom*—Wigglesworth, whose diary is an abysmal lament of his filth, guilt, brutishness, harlotry, with some of it written in code—well, my point is, it seems a waste and a denial of the liberating truth that to be in Christ is to be a new creature. "Old things are passed away. Behold, all things are made new" (2 Cor. 5:17).

I like that word *behold*. It prolongs the gaze. I need a long, favorable gaze because lately I'm seeing Dostoevsky's "vaudeville of devils" within my depths. The Puritans are right. My dentist is right. I need to correct my bite; wear the splint; eat smaller helpings; be happy with my wardrobe; show love to small, rude people; care less about being thanked, and bundle myself with all my botchwork into my closet of prayer. That's where *he* is, in the small, private space, not needing the limelight, loving me as I am, reason enough to want to be like him.

LETHAL SHADOW

I've been in a lethal shadow for a long time, and it's the shadow of someone I deeply love. This is where the book I'm reading says I'm supposed to work out my salvation—right at the point of suffering—but I confess I haven't worked it out very well, and sometimes I wonder if at all. Sometimes I think I'm wearing a God mask, walking around with the trappings of faith and fooling everyone, especially myself. The truth is, there's great unease at heart, a shattered confidence, and I find the work of praying and believing to be difficult, in the same way exercise is hard, or falling asleep. I have come to see that one can follow the idea of God while being far from him, can live in a kind of spiritual February where days are lit with washed-out light and there is no sense of spring.

And then it comes to me—the way it did when Wayne and I were camping, and I looked through the tent opening and saw that the dark, fascinating sky being brushed by wind-tossed branches overhead, had, when I shut my eyes, turned suddenly and imperceptibly light—in this same way, grace alters existence. A bright sky emerges and the shriveled landscape of the heart is freshened. I stumbled out of the tent into a new day. There is always this possibility of renewal in the resurrection of Jesus Christ—I hold it now for me and for the child of my tears.

TANGY CHERMOULA

"It's not about how big the lever is that I'm pushing on. That's always going to feel very small. But I believe there's grace at work—a kind of a tailwind behind what I do. However small my work may start out, God is going to multiply what's really good in my work in ways that may end up being huge over generations or centuries."

I'm chewing on these words of Andy Crouch, even as I taste the tangy chermoula sauce that will marinate what was a big club of squash that took an hour of hard labor to halve, scrape, peel, and dice before I browned it in olive oil. A small, good work, this meal of my making. Besides the butternut squash, we will have a gratin of salmon and spinach, and enjoy easy talk as we eat by candlelight on a Wednesday night after a full day's work at our jobs. Not every meal I fix is complex, but every meal is fresh and requires time, precious time, to prepare.

Perhaps the tailwind behind this is my prayer for such fragrant moments to fill the homes of neighbors everywhere, for the slow simmer of time to do its work and teach us to eschew the quick and the fake for the whole and real and risen, like a freshly baked loaf of bread, laughter in the mouths of those around the table, or the unseen Host who invites us to taste his goodness.

URL-Y TO BED

Speaking in tongues of technology leaves a bad taste in my mouth. Blog, for example: a perfect pig of a word that calls for an ugh as in ughly. And then there are the acronyms, clicked off as if they were *real* words: URLs, ISPs, RADs and VOIPs. How about retweet and twaffic? Are you getting that queasy sensation yet? I've been to the webinar and found it wanting. So do the teleconference hosts, apparently, for sometimes they give in to a nostalgic urge to let drop a word or phrase referring to the ordinary world of tree and sky.

I attended an Email Newsletter Optimization seminar where the presenter—an overly-enthusiastic woman with long, graying hair—used the phrase "low-hanging fruit" and my heart leapt up—but only for a nanosecond, for sadly, I discovered she was using it to refer to the most accessible features on her pixelated page. Set as it was among non-words in a conversation about SEOs and change-tracking functionality, the fruit was about as tasty as the dollhouse ham in Beatrix Potter's *Tale of Two Bad Mice*. No thank you. I'll take my fruit from a poem like Keats' "Eve of St. Agnes":

> And still she slept an azure-lidded sleep,
> In blanched linen, smooth, and lavender'd,

While he from forth the closet brought a heap
Of candied apple, quince, and plum, and gourd,
With jellies smoother than the creamy curd,
And lucent syrups, tinct with cinnamon;
Manna and dates, in argosy transferr'd
From Fez; and spiced dainties, every one,
From silken Samarcand to cedar'd Lebanon.

For at least the fruit in a poem refers to that which exists in the tangible world—to orbs of sweet, fleshy succulence—while the words of cyberspace refer to—what? Bytes, ASCIs, hypertext, nodes, MIMES, and jpegs—all virtual, of course, meaning "not physically existing but made to appear by software." Letters without words, words without souls, geek talk being mainstreamed, and ultimately the incarnational nature of language being reduced to the gibberish of gifs and G-zips. Such a bloodless lexicon is not to be confused with the colorful slang of truck drivers alerting their buddies to "bears in the air" and "disco lights," nor with lunch counter waiters calling out orders to the cooks of "bloodhounds in the hay" and "cowboys with spurs." No, the language of the machine has no root beyond itself, and indeed, no root at all, needing not even a wire anymore to connect us to our absence.

WHERE MUSIC COMES FROM

On this gilded, good morning, seated by my window, I would like to shout my joy to the world, for I am soaring on the wind of a resplendent choral piece suggested by my son: *Sicut cervus desiderat*—"As the deer longs for running water . . ."

I felt the stirring the other night at a concert featuring a Ugandan artist named Samite. With a variety of native instruments, he piped and plucked sounds of the forest—the awakening birds and monkeys, his grandfather's flute, the sorrow of trees lost to cities. I sensed the shadows melting as he moved with his eyes closed and shoulders swaying, his lithe body rounding the spaces about him.

When I think about the power of music, a passage from Kafka's *Metamorphosis* comes to mind. Gregor, transformed into a dung beetle, risks death just to be near his sister's violin playing: "Was he an animal, that music should move him so? He felt as if the way to the unknown nourishment he longed for were coming to light."

It was the nourishment of my daughter Katy's pure, crystalline voice singing "Silent Night" at a nursing home many years ago that moved one man among the many in wheelchairs to raise his hand again and again.

TIDEPOOLS

Music filled my heart in eighth grade chorus until I thought it would burst as we sang "How Lovely Is Thy Dwelling Place." We stood on risers in the gym with all the windows open, and I remember a bird flew over and began to sing too.

It was a throbbing bluegrass rhythm at a famous music shed in southwest Virginia known as the Carter Fold that drew us to come down from our seats to the dance floor where we flat-footed (or faked it) and twirled and laughed, locking arms—children and yuppies and farmers and students and old folks on the floor moving faster and faster as the banjo and fiddles quickened their tempo, and we were one jubilant sea. But what stirred me most was seeing a large, dark-haired woman stomping and swinging her legs with such reckless abandon it seemed as if the dance floor and pulsing music belonged to her alone. And then I realized she was blind. The joy on her face when she raised it struck me full force. It was a resurrection moment: all that light from one who lives in the dark.

GLASS MUSIC

I heard a sound that was new in the world, flowing from the large, petal-shaped amplifiers of a hand-made instrument known as the Cristal Baschet. The musician rubs moistened fingers along glass rods, producing a low, piping music that carries one imaginatively to the damp stone interior of a cathedral. The inventors of this and many other fascinating musical sculptures are two French brothers, Francois and Bernard Baschet, both in their nineties and still creating.

The brothers and their sonorously-serious playthings— how they bless me! How I cheer them on—I, not even sixty, finding myself doubting at the most unwelcome moments, the grace and the gift to play my flute of words.

WAXWINGS

1.

How is it that day after day the hedges stand unruffled, the street remains the street, my rising and dressing and driving and sitting at my desk go on as always and I am lulled into thinking that it will always be this way, that the Swiss music box on my bedside table given by my father to my mother to me will keep its three secret tunes forever. But then I wake up one spring morning to find the hedge swooning with wings as the birds have arrived, swooping down from heaven to gorge on holly berries. It goes on for three days—the ruddy robins and lemon-gray cedar waxwings streaking the canvas of air, creating three new mornings as I wheel my car out into the world with the spectacular dance falling off my rearview mirror.

2.

Just as the ordinary can explode into ecstasy, so does it sometimes flatten to doom. That's how it was when my mother rode to her death, beginning with an early morning and the usual cereal and coffee, and a waiting, warming car that carried her to the hospital for her first treatment. Her husband, John, had the papers.

Together they walked expectantly down the hall to the room with the chair, the comfy chemo chair. It was all routine. They followed instructions. They did this for three straight mornings, to be repeated over time. Between the black drips were nausea and weakness, falling, failing, balding, babbling—my God, it went on too long, the poisoning and scalding until the last ride home to bed where, on the night before she died, she rose up at 3 a.m., according to the hospice nurse, to wave at Jesus. On those nights, John was sitting on a stool serenading her with the old songs they loved.

I wrote an elegy to her and chose the most difficult of forms, the sestina, because hers was the most difficult of lives, and she, a glamorous, intelligent, funny, faith-filled, loving woman, over-came every enemy.

Death, This Day

She rose and dressed as if the day were harmless,
her heart a steady heart. The car chimed on.
Her husband found the streets had kept their angles
and led her to the room of sterile stations:
the padded chair, the seat of transformation,
with lines to hold her steady through the quaking.

Her mind draws back to heavens darkly quaking.
A cow awash in rain stands fixed and harmless,
but then the stabbing light, the transformation
from form to bellowing fire. The clock chimes on.
Her father turns the knob to find a station.
Her mother's carrot peelings fall at angles.

Time moves fast, like one who chased *her* angles.
Hands on hips, she set his soul to quaking.
The war was on, he wrote from many stations,

named her Duchess, claimed his love was harmless.
Marriage and arms, the grieving bells chimed on
as if to call the truce that transformed nations.

The newly shattered world of transformation
exposed her in a maze of broken angles.
The children needed bread, their cries chimed on.
She knocked on doors—the city left her quaking,
longing for home—the fields, green and harmless,
the patient faces. She bundled to the station.

But now she shudders in her final station.
The blight inside has wrought a transformation
no one believes—to see her lying harmless
as a shorn lamb, tubes running at all angles,
her daughters telling her, with voices quaking,
to hold on, hold as the shallow breath chimes on.

Outside, spring stirs, the mourning doves chime on.
The sun lingers at each budding station,
lighting the blades of grass, the green flames quaking,
the night shift blinking at the transformation
from pallid halls to the dogwoods' bright angles,
with sleep ahead, when time is held harmless

and unseen stars chime on. All transformations
are but shifts of station. So, let angels
loose. Let quaking end. Death, this day, is harmless.

3.

How to think about my country: to watch it being dismantled
day by dizzying day, to see banks faltering and failing, jobs
and businesses folding, national leaders lying, human life being

reduced to economic formulas—all this as the sky goes on being blue.

When do I reckon the tipping point that requires me to adopt what Bruno Bettelheim called "crisis thinking"? Bettelheim, a Holocaust survivor and child psychologist who, sadly, committed suicide in 1990 and whose reputation has suffered in recent years, nonetheless offered insight into why people fail to recognize impending disaster. I quote Carol Bly, from her essay, "Bruno Bettelheim: Three Ideas to Try in Madison, Minnesota":

Even when the Germans began arresting Jews in the 1930s, many of the Jews refused to leave Germany because the aura of their possessions—the rooms, the rugs, the paintings—gave them a sense of normalcy in things: they'd projected some of themselves into these objects around them, so if the objects were still there, surely everything was usual? What they needed to do was to switch to crisis thinking: they needed to say to themselves, "This is not business as usual. We must run away at night, or join the Underground, or separate and plan to meet in Switzerland."

Bettelheim says we must speak or fight, whichever is called for, at the first moment of our anxiety. National Socialism looked like "business as usual" in 1932 and 1933; by 1934 it was too late. To speak in America has become difficult; the air in the public forum is viciously political. To fight might mean joining the Underground, but where and what is it?

The cars drive up and down. The rugs and lamps remain. How easy it is to be duped by what Camus called "blind human faith in the near future." For the near future obscures the far country of the soul and the light that shows us how to live faithfully, no matter what plague may come.

FROWN

What am I to make of a church that watches paralytic souls being let down into the suffocating sanctuary with Jesus said to be in the midst, but with no healing to show for it? Instead, a list of requirements is put before the cripple, like links in a crushing chain. "We will help you if . . ." but the if is a chasm too wide and deep for crossing, and the paralytic, now ruled a rebel by the righteous assembly, despairs of ever walking again, much less finding a hollow in the Lord's body to lay his head.

Behind their frowning Providence Is—a frown.

MERMAID'S TEARS

I always liked sea glass for its own sake and, collecting it over many years and shores, I imagined it as bits of broken sky or shattered rainbows. The only tutelage I received in my scavenging was from my son, who once suggested that much of what I was stuffing into my coat pockets was broken beer bottles. So, I became more discriminating, selecting only frosty glass with smooth edges as I continued to fill my bowl with gems.

But then I read a book and lost my innocence. The author, a sea glass specialist, explained how some pieces are worth more than others. Sea glass is ranked in value by color (brown, Kelly green and clear are common; jade and amber, less common; cobalt blue and milk white, very uncommon, etc.) and by type—there is production glass (soda bottles, for example) and the more valuable designer glass (from artistic objects). Suddenly, my private pleasure in spying glints of color among the seashells no longer satisfied. Now I must have the extremely rare, the most sought after, the red, the black. Indeed, I found myself scouring rather than combing the shore, and that is when I saw my greed and repented, recognizing that entire empires rise and fall on such plunder and that the kaleidoscope sea would freely and always give me treasure.

HEART HOLLOW

What lives in a hollow? Sometimes something, sometimes nothing. With a tree hollow, you can't always tell because it's dark all the way down. With a heart hollow, it's the same. You can't always tell, especially when it's your own heart.

A wise counselor has been helping me to see better, see a frightened shape hiding in the depths. I begin to recognize it, my own true guilt. I've kept it padded and protected, fed with good reasons for what I did and why I didn't. I've got to hand it to blind old Oedipus. There was nobility in his facing who he was as he hunted down his unbearable truth. Blame it on Fate if you like, he was still an actor in the grotesque drama. In acknowledging his guilt, he became fully a man—though a wretched one, stumbling about on the earth.

So it is I am beginning to find courage to confront myself, not as one sinned against, but as a woman who like Oedipus came to forking roads and chose poorly. The results have been costly and far-flung. No wonder I hid from the knowing. How can any of us comprehend the effects of a given action or inaction, whether an impulsive word, a disapproving look, an awkward intervention, a small hesitation. If we knew, oh Lord if we knew, we might well gouge out our eyes or hang ourselves. But ten words spoken from a lonely height altered the plane of our mortal life and made freedom possible. Ten words clothed our bald ignorance and iniquity—"Father, forgive them, for they know not what they do"—so that against the backdrop of those bleeding, stretched out, pinned down arms, we can, we must confess everything.

A ROYAL SEASON MIXED
WITH MYRRH

1.

The shore is a serendipitous place where the world's oddments land and find themselves entangled in community with other displaced things.

On a crisp December day, Wayne and I were walking by the bay when we noticed in the distance a large, spreading shape. As we approached, we saw that it was the root system and half-trunk of a huge tree, washed up on its side and decorated in an unusual way by invisible hands. On shaggy roots were hung a sock, a pair of sunglasses, an empty Pepsi can. We looked around for ornaments to add—Serendipity! A light bulb half buried in sand would do nicely. So would a feather, a clump of seaweed. I liked this game very much. I liked being numbered with stragglers who knew a Christmas tree when they saw one, out there, stranded, far from any forest but a tree nonetheless fit for embellishment at a time of year when all the disjunct souls of the world are looking for a limb.

2.

My mother's hardworking hands were beautiful—mending, smoothing, basting, trimming, typing, page-turning, weed-pulling hands, and they were never put to more important use than at Christmas. There was little money for buying gifts, but Mom's creative and resourceful mind sprung plans that called for late nights (after putting her three girls to bed) at her sewing machine or the dining room table with scissors, glue, fabric, paint. She crinkled and molded the varieties of wrapping paper and ribbons to fit her creations and happily watched our faces on Christmas morning as we tore open the packages to find a doll cradle made from a bread basket or hand-made dresses for our Barbies.

For the years of my girlhood I maintained a scrapbook and each December recorded "What I Got for Christmas." Sometimes there were only three or four presents, but I don't remember ever feeling deprived. Each gift added much to my life—the home-made pajamas, the dirndl skirt with slightly uneven hem. After I grew up and had my own children, she continued to send gifts—a stuffed turtle with button eyes, a puffy baby quilt. She took great delight in thinking about the gift in terms of the child, and this, along with the weeks of preparation and work that went into her idea of Christmas, stirred something deep in my heart and stirs me still as I think of her and feel the ache of her absence.

These reflections bring to mind the love of God, so evident in my mother. He shapes his blessings with each child in mind. But his greatest gift—salvation through his son, Jesus Christ—is the most wondrous and costly gift in the universe: "The gift of God is eternal life through Jesus Christ our Lord" (Rom. 6:23). All praise and thanksgiving belong to God who freely gives and invites us freely to receive.

Advent

Through the needle's eye the rich man came,
squeezing through stars of razor light
that pared his body down to thread.

Gravity crushed his heart's chime
and the breath that breathed out worlds
now flattened as fire between walls.
The impossible slit stripped him,
admitting him to stitch the human breach.

3.

How is it that any given moment holds the world's big history
and my small one, so that the new moment is impossibly old?
I was sitting in church this morning, contemplating the Incar-
nation and how my moment of holding that thought had been
expanding since the start of time, since before there was time,
and the weight of the Lord's love broke open in my heart like a
sweet, heavy fragrance. I wept knowing there is no true joy on
earth without sorrow and that the incense of this royal season is
mixed with myrrh.

I've left my family far behind. My feet have their own life, taking me away and away. The naked beach curves like a woman's body. Watery hands clasp and free my ankles. Sandpipers look in mirrors left by the last wave. In the distance, sky and sand are one and I am going there, drawn by the vastness of Being. I exalt in immensity but there's also this loneliness, Lord, like an ache in my bones. Please give me a sign. I know it's outrageous to ask, but how about a sand dollar? You know how much I like them.

I chide myself for such a prayer as this. The Word tells me God is everywhere at once but here everywhere is swallowed up in roaring. Against the sheen of the infinite shore, I see the motions of my life carrying but the weight of a ghost crab. I've seen no sand dollars on this beach and barely any shells, but look, here it is at my feet—a flower floated down from heaven. I pick it up and study the star at the center drawn like a hieroglyph from another world. Yes, I'm with you, says the sign. I turn back the way I came, awed by the wealth in my hand.

SKETCHES OF HOME
Suzanne Underwood Rhodes

Before you do some writing of your own, let me mention a foundational principle of writing which hopefully you have already learned in school. It is the virtue of conciseness. A skillful writer cuts the fat and thickens the gravy. Cutting the fat means using strong nouns and verbs and omitting excessive adjectives, adverbs, clichés, trite speech, and fillers like "a really pretty girl." Thickening the gravy means choosing words that are richly suggestive: "Death's second self that seals up all in rest."

In poetry, conciseness is taken farther than in prose (sentences and paragraphs). Written in LINES where individual words are highly visible, the language is much compressed. In a poem, "there is really so little room," writes Sylvia Plath. "So little time!" Poems make Plath "think of those round glass Victorian paperweights . . . a clear globe, self-complete, very pure, with a forest or village or family group within it. You turn it upside down, then back. It snows. Everything is changed in a minute. It will never be the same in there—not the fir trees, nor the gables, nor the faces." Another name for this compression is density. Think of density as a loaf of whole-grain bread taken straight from the oven. It is thick and hearty, tasting faintly of molasses. Lines of poems should be like this, full of rich details and meaningful ingredients.

THE ROAR ON THE OTHER SIDE
A Guide for Student Poets
Suzanne Underwood Rhodes

www.ingramcontent.com/pod-product-compliance
Lightning Source LLC
Chambersburg PA
CBHW051732040426
42447CB00008B/1102